The Societal Evolution of Male Stereotypes

Gender Bashing of Men in America

By: James M. Lowrance © 2011

To all of the men and women, who faithfully fulfill their roles of leadership, parenting and spousal duties in today's society.

3

TABLE OF CONTENTS:

INTRODUCTION:

If I were to sum up the central point in two sentences, for addressing this sensitive subject within the chapters of this book, I would say this:

"When a negative trait or practice is generally and entirely attributed to a people of a particular race, gender or origin, it is an unfair generalization that we call a 'stereotype'. When it manifests unchallenged and unanswered, it can over time cause society to lose respect for a particular people as a whole or to an extent, for society itself."

In some cases, those who might not agree with these statements or who might not understand why I attempt to counter-balance the stereotyping trend, in my own small way, may at the same time, listen to the very things I am addressing but from the wrong (stereotypical) perspectives and they will see no problem in it. Others may not like to hear the issue expressed from any perspective but would rather see things run their course whether they are positive or negative in nature.

I would suggest that if a person doesn't appreciate the subject matter being pointed out, in-general, simply don't read or listen to materials relating to it. It's that simple! For those who do see the importance in addressing aspects of this subject, it is for this reason; they are worth expressing in my opinion.

It is my hope that readers of the chapters that follow will find balance and perspective brought to those aspects of gender stereotypes that will be addressed, following.

CHAPTER ONE

Why Write on Gender Stereotypes?

In some cases, people have grown so accustomed to hearing stereotypes in regard to sexual behaviors attributed to men that they actually believe them and expect everyone to continue going along with them (i.e. men think about sex every 52 seconds). If everyone does continue to go along with them however, without expressing opinions to counterbalance them or to bring better perspective to them, as has been the case in years past, balance will not be brought to the subject of male sexual stereotypes (nor to those directed at females).

I am not the only one who has recognized this trend, thankfully and there are others out there trying to counterbalance the long running sexual stereotypes that exist. Research on any online search-engine using key works such as "sexual stereotypes", "male bashing", "gender stereotypes" etc..., will yield evidence that I am far from alone in seeing how damaging and unfair these trends are that have been continued and built upon for decades.

To offer an immediate example; a few months ago, I heard a woman on the panel of a Christian television talk show repeat a once commonly-heard phrase, saying that "all men are basically pigs". No one else on the panel reacted with any disagreement, in pointing out that while **some men** are pigs, **all men** are not. This was similar to a media event not many years ago, in which it was stated that "men just don't get it", in reference to men being too moronic to resist the practice of sexually harassing women they come in contact with. A better statement would have been to say that "some men just don't get it".

Personal experience is one area I have not written about in much detail up to this point but experiences in my youth, I believe are what triggered my desire to see balance brought to the male sexual stereotype subject. While growing up, I witnessed repeated, one-sided reporting about the male side of deviant sexual behavior and moronic gender role-playing. It was often applied to the entire male gender in-general, rather than it being stated that these behaviors are present in "a percent of males" or in certain ones and not representative of all males generally.

I also noticed that the vast majority of the time, in these type discussions, the female gender was not implemented in committing any sexually deviant behaviors or for imbalanced gender-role playing. This despite the fact, that it is obvious that a percent of women do perpetrate these type things, although at statistically lower incidence compared to males.

The Talk Show Venue

I observed for years that when sexually deviant or moronic behaviors by females was occasionally included in discussions on talk shows I viewed during my youth in the 1970s, the studio-audience would react uncomfortably and were seemingly offended at times. They were far more tolerant however, when the subject matter pertained to male perpetrators, possibly because it offered opportunity to vent frustration towards males in general, rather than toward perpetrators in-general. The fact is however, that it is not proper to generalize males or females in such discussions because this fails to give opportunity to recognize the fact that there are respectable people found within both genders.

Why, is this sometimes not recognized or acknowledged even today, so that these type discussions are better-balanced, rather than gravitating toward gender stereotypes?

I personally believe that among other reasons, protection of the female gender and reputation was actually part of the reason behind less discussion regarding females who fall within the perpetrator categories. It was not considered proper or respectful to discuss the percent of females who practiced deviant sexual or moronic behaviors. This was especially true of those subjects that had potential for creating more embarrassment for them in recognizing that those of their own gender do indeed commit these type things.

It was seemingly more acceptable in years past, to discuss sexually deviant practices in females, if it pertained to the "empowering types" of behaviors. What do I mean by this? I am referring to things such as prostitution (please excuse the bluntness) and gold-digging, in-which women entice willing men through sex, to pay them money. This is actually recognized by some observers as a form of power.

It is also sometimes recognized as a form of power, to discuss how women lure men into viewing pornography by participating in its production or even into marriage for money.

Women are Intelligent and Responsible

Certainly there is also such a thing as women who are forced into these type lifestyles but implying that all of them are, is to also imply that women are weak-minded and have no will of their own, which is yet another stereotype. These type subjects were fair-game for discussion on the talk shows of years past but if you brought up the subject of female child molesters or women who developed porn addictions or sexual addictions in general, as some men do, you often saw audiences react unfavorably toward the subject having been brought up.

Not-so however, as long as male perpetrators were the subject. The media-trend specialists knew this and they also knew that the viewing audience was predominantly female and this is partly what took the talk shows into these directions.

It was also partly my experiences growing up that revealed to me that females can also be perpetrators of deviant and moronic type behaviors as mentioned previously but no one seemed to be pointing this out when discussing this subject-matter, from my observation.

When I was age 5 years old, I was repeatedly fondled by a teenage girl who touched parts of my body that were supposed to be off-limits. Who knows, if I was a bit older and both of us being minors, it might have been consensual but as it was, it was unwelcome by me. My mother became aware of this, after I reacted with crying on an occasion when I was told I was going to have to be babysat by this girl. Upon my mother questioning the girl, she admitted to what she had been doing and apologized to us. Later when I reached the age of 8 years a teen male neighbor perpetrated sexual deviance on me as well. He forced me repeatedly to watch his private part in an aroused state and then forced me to talk about it. Thankfully the abuse didn't go further than this. He perpetrated this behavior on me by forcing me to go into his garage alone with him.

Because of my past experience in being forced to submit to being repeatedly fondled as a younger child, I told my mother about it and she spoke to the boy's mother, who promptly put a stop to it.

When I was in my preteens, a friend's mother attempted to get me to fool around with her and I had to literally, physically struggle to get away from her. My friend, whose mother attempted this, had walked in on her fooling around with his uncle on one occasion, which embarrassed him beyond description and in my belief, also devastated him. Another same-age friend of mine told me this same woman had indecently exposed herself to him and because of my own experience with her, I knew he was not lying about it.

Also during my teen years, an older adult female sexually harassed me by repeatedly referring to my private parts and asking me if I was touching them. I was incredibly humiliated by this and this gained me an early understanding of how degraded one can feel, who is sexually harassed. She enjoyed seeing my embarrassment and humiliation. I don't necessarily believe it was for sexual gratification on her part but still very improper regardless.

The Drive but not the Courage

I had a girlfriend (2 years older than I) when I was age 15, who wanted me to have relations with her but I was inexperienced and terrified of embarrassment if I performed incorrectly had I participated, plus I was afraid of the consequences that could result if I did follow-through with it. She resorted to showing me pornography at one point, in attempting to interest me and while I definitely had the drive, I did not have the guts to oblige her.

Now 30 years later and being in my late 40s and having been married for nearly 30 years to a wonderful woman and having two grown children of my own, a boy and a girl, I'm thankful for the choice of abstinence I made in my youth. In the past few years I've seen other men not so fortunate in their marriages. I witnessed a onetime close friend of mine as well as witnessing one of my nephews lose their wives due to them having porn addictions that escalated into their having sex with men they were meeting through the internet. If you only observe the coverage on these issues by the media, you might tend to believe these things only happen with the genders reversed.

From the above examples of my personal experiences I realized early in life that they do happen from both sides.

Why some Men won't Report Sex Offenders

As a man, I bring up these experiences because women have been attesting to their experiences in these areas for many years, freely and in detail but men seldom do. There is a stigma that says men who relate experiences such as molestation or harassment that has been perpetrated upon them by females are wimps for doing so. It is for this reason that even under-aged males do not report or talk about their experiences with female sex offenders.

You may note that adult women who were apprehended for having relations with under aged males as covered in recent news coverage, were not often discovered because the male victims reported it but because their parents eventually caught on to it. Some say it is "every boy's dream" to have such experiences (a stereotypical view) but this is not what mental health experts are reporting.

The experts rather point-out that there are serious after-effects these experiences have on most male victims that they may carry for the rest of their lives.

The fear of being accused of being homosexual for not enjoying such an experience is yet another reason straight men will not relate these types of experiences that have happened to them. This is especially true if the offenders were also males. Regardless of stigmas, I do not believe it is right and okay for females to talk about sexual abuse they have experienced but wrong for men to do so. Both should come forward without fear for doing so because of the possible stereotypes that might be applied to their experiences by ignorant people. Hindering, rather than encouraging victims to come-forward, only serves to place people into a type of bondage that keeps them from receiving any needed counseling.

Women are Wonderful

I also have the common sense to know that just because of my few negative experiences with females, this does not mean that all of them are doing these type things because the majority of them are not. Nor do I hold unforgiveness or grudges against anyone.

The Societal Evolution of Male Stereotypes

I have the intelligence to know that there are wonderful, beautiful (inward and outward) women, who are quality human beings that are an asset to their gender and to the human race. There are women who show respect and who also deserve to be respected. It would be nice to see this same type realization more often, when the roles are reversed.

Women who have observed these type behaviors in men or have had these type things perpetrated upon them, should also recognize that some men are respectful and worthy of respect. You would not think this balanced recognition exists when hearing some women seemingly attributing these type things to the entire male gender. While this type view does not take away our abilities as men, to be respected fathers and husbands it certainly does not lend toward it.

I'm not saying this is an easy attitude to adapt when one has negative experiences by several members of a gender. Some people experience terrible things at the hands of other people but we absolutely must not let it cause us to lose faith in others who are of the human race. If we do, it can only be down hill for us from there because we live in a world of both male and female.

The Societal Evolution of Male Stereotypes

Everyone is capable of both good and bad but it's what we choose to do through properly guided morals that make us who we are.

It is each person's choice to participate or to refrain-from the degradation called stereotyping and gender bashing. I personally have made a choice in my life not to participate in gender generalizing but rather to bring balance to the issue when possible.

CHAPTER TWO

Female Sex Offenders

(Sexual Abuse has no Gender Barriers)

With a number of events involving female child molesters in recent years being covered in the media, including a second round of sexual harassment and molestation charges against females arising from a girl's school established by a famous female celebrity, I felt the need to include a chapter regarding societal issues as related to female sex offenders.

There are still those who offer excuses for woman who are perpetrators of sexual deviance toward minors and this is disturbing because it implies that they are somehow not responsible for their own actions. It also implies that women are less-responsible or less-intelligent than are men.

As I have mentioned in past articles I've written on this subject, I recognize the fact that men are perpetrators of sexually deviant behaviors including harassment of females, far more often than are women.

Despite this fact however, women are perpetrators often enough that it is no longer considered rare in incidence. Some statistics state that approximately 8% of reported sexual abuse is committed by woman. Statistics are somewhat skewed however, by a variety of factors, including the fact that male victims are less-willing to report sexual abuse by females due to stigmas that might be attached by doing so (i.e. accusations implying that only males who are wimps or homosexuals resist sexual advances by women).

Disturbing Statistics

Some statistics for the U.S. and other countries state that a large percent of female sexual abuse is perpetrated upon their own children. These are facts difficult to recognize or to openly discuss but hiding from them will not make them go away. More education on the subject is in-fact key to prevention. Children for example should not be instructed to only avoid "strange men" but should be instructed to avoid "strangers, in-general", regardless of gender.

Employers for another example should not be less-willing to consider reports from males who are sexually harassed by females than for incidences of the reverse scenario.

Within my own small circle of family for example, both my son and my older brother have worked at government funded facilities in two different states, both being youth detention centers and both having seen female workers terminated for sexual harassment of fellow-employees and for having relations with detainees.

No Excuse is Acceptable

I was impressed by a well-known female news media spokesperson who has covered child abuse cases on her program who recently corrected a female psychiatrist when she stated that in the case of female sex abusers, their behaviors are generally caused by emotional problems. She responded to the statement by asking the psychiatrists to not offer this excuse to a recent female perpetrator who sexually abused and also murdered her victim.

Not long ago, psychiatrists were also stating that female teachers who abuse under-age male students did-so because their husbands were emotionally absent from them and were not providing them proper love and nurturing in the home.

Could it not be said that <u>anyone</u> who sexually abuses has emotional problems or is seeking some type of fulfillment they have been deprived-of? Does this type excuse keep male perpetrators from being punished for their crimes against minor victims? The fact is that deviant sexual behaviors do not have gender barriers that they do not cross. Abusive behaviors are perpetrated by males, females, large people and small people, those who are rich and poor and by every imaginable category of age-responsible human beings. Not recognizing this fact is pure naivety and sometimes non-recognition of it seems to be purposeful for whatever reasons. It is possible that some who offer excuses for offenders of a specific type may believe they are defending their sex, their particular profession or their status in society, by downplaying the deviant acts of their peers.

On the other hand, I personally believe with firm conviction that it is also wrong to stereotype genders by implying for example, that "all men" are sexual harassers or abusers or that "all female teachers" are capable of seeking improper relationships with young male students. Does this type generalizing still happen in current times? It certainly does and we have decades of ongoing practice that has continued these ideas.

Movements that took Wrong Turns

Some sincere movements of the past, whose goals were to defend against sexual stereotyping and oppression ended in the movements themselves becoming one of gender bashing. This eventually backfired on them, due to a lack of balance and has taken decades for society to even partially recover from.

It's time to get real when it comes to educating the public about sexual abuse of all types. It's a difficult subject but one, we must face if we are going to see gains made against it for future generations. Letting sexual stereotypes and gender movements get in the way of recognizing the reality of the problem will only hinder any solutions made toward it now and in the future.

CHAPTER THREE

Men Who Hate Women

(Hating the Opposite Sex)

There is an episode of the "Little Rascals" series when Spanky and Alfalfa formed a club called the "He-Man Woman-Haters Club" and all that joined had to take an oath never to have anything to do with females. The episode is humorous because the boys find after a while that it becomes impossible not to have anything to do with girls and they begin to go behind each others back, breaking their oaths to do so.

Recently, I was talking to a lady manager with a company I previously did contract sales for and she brought up the fact that her straight daughter, who is in college and seeking to eventually enter her desired profession, wants nothing to do with men. My wife who was present at the time of this conversation asked her if she had been in some way hurt by a young man and this mom stated that she felt that this was indeed the case.

The Societal Evolution of Male Stereotypes

A Reality Check

Ever so often, you'll hear a member of one of the sexes, state that they literally hate those of the opposite sex and want nothing to do with them. Some cases are extreme and some do indeed have a sad or tragic reason behind them. Despite this fact, there are several undeniable truths that both genders must admit because they will find it very difficult to get along in this world if they truly seek to avoid the opposite sex. I will even go so far as to say most will find it impossible and they need to give their selves a reality check, so that they can go forward with life and not live in unhappiness and restriction.

First of all, both sexes are capable of causing hurt, pain and tragedy to others of the opposite sex, their same sex and virtually anyone they come in contact with. What we can't allow this to do to us is to create a negatively judgmental view of everyone who is their peer, in regard to sex, age group, race etc... This is unfair to them and is especially unfair to one's self because it can cause lost opportunities to connect with truly wonderful people of both genders who certainly do exist in the world.

The Societal Evolution of Male Stereotypes

Our Undeniable Interconnectedness

The reality is that both sexes are undeniably interconnected with each other and there is nothing that can change this fact no matter how much one may want to. Each of us is born through the union of a male and female and what we each become, comes from both our mothers and our fathers. When you look at it scientifically, the female chromosome comes from the male sperm (XX-chromosome) and without it, female babies are not created. Woman who claim to hate men are, hating, what is a part of them and the same is true of men who claim to hate women. Men have been heard to claim hatred of women and yet they are for lack of a better term, a "product of the womb". Much of what a man becomes is passed down to him from his mother, as well as from his father.

This is the "reality check" I mentioned earlier. When people are somehow led down the path of hatred toward the opposite sex, it could actually be recognized as a mental or emotional complex of some type. The reality of their thinking has been seriously affected by negative events or negative impressions they have experienced.

Admittedly, such events can be tragic and when they do cause people to develop hatred complexes, they are in need of counseling that re-instills these facts of life within them. In some cases, people are actually mentally ill and can be affected in this area of male or female hate-complexes. When actual mental illness is present or develops, it has led to people committing violence or even murders and afterward claiming it was due to their hatred for those of the opposite gender. This is tragic but true and news media occasionally reports on cases of "black widow" type females and "jack the ripper" type males.

We must remember that no matter how tragic or hurtful an event may be, that has been perpetrated upon us by the member of a gender, we cannot judge everyone of that same sex, for the actions of one or even for the actions of many within the group (prejudice). The same is true of race, religion and any other diversity we find within the human race.

In Touch with Both Sides

We are all part of each other and though we may mentally separate from each other at times, we cannot do so in reality.

27

While each of us is distinctly male or female, we all carry traits of both sexes, given to us by our parents. You may have heard people say that men should get in touch with their female or feminine side and women should do so in regard to their masculine side and while this is not always a comfortable idea, there is some truth to that statement. Medical science shows that males carry female hormones and females carry male hormones but each in different balance. Women have testosterone and men have estrogen but the different balance in these and other hormones and in the reproductive organs are part of what makes each of us, who we are.

Adam's Rib

If we look at it from the perspective of the Holy Bible for example, we see the first-ever medical surgery performed by God himself. He causes a "deep sleep" to fall upon Adam (sounds much-like a reference to anesthesia) and extracts one of his ribs, to create a woman.

Genesis 2:21: *"And the LORD God caused a deep sleep to fall upon Adam, and he slept: and he took one of his ribs, and closed up the flesh instead thereof"*

God then creates the woman from the rib of the man.

Genesis 2:22-23: *"Then the rib which the LORD God had taken from man He made into a woman, and He brought her to the man. And Adam said: "This is now bone of my bones And flesh of my flesh; She shall be called Woman, Because she was taken out of Man."*

Afterward, all men were born of women and Adam recognized that the woman (Eve) was literally his own flesh and blood. When a man joins to a woman in marriage, he is in essence taking back that rib, into his body.

Ephesians 5:31: *"For this cause shall a man leave his father and mother, and shall be joined unto his wife, and they two shall be one flesh."*

Separating ourselves from the opposite sex? In reality that's not even possible in the true sense of leaving no trace within us of those who pro-created us. This is an important fact of life that we would all do well not to forget.

CHAPTER FOUR

Unrealistic Sexual Stereotypes

I was watching an interview show on a Christian television program I enjoy and whose host I respect a great deal. On this particular program, he was interviewing two men and one woman, on the subject of sexual promiscuity and reasons why each of the sexes indulge in this type behavior. The female panelist, who has also authored a book on the subject was being interviewed and came across as very sincere and wanting to make honest and helpful points on the subject. She still managed however, to include some stereotypical views about males and females in the interview.

It should be pointed out that stereotypes always have elements of truth within them but a better definition for stereotypes, is to describe them as being imbalanced or exaggerated versions of the truth. They lack perspective in other words, as previously mentioned and are usually simply over-generalized views of real issues.

I want to address a few of these that were stated on this talk show program because I felt they were stated by this woman, in ways that lacked the balance and perspective that was needed.

The Societal Evolution of Male Stereotypes

This in my opinion placed them in the overly-generalized category or "stereotypes" category.

The Promiscuity Question

The first one I want to address was her response to the question by the host-interviewer, as to why some women become promiscuous with their bodies. Her response started out by making the point that women are taught early in life and conditioned to believe they are supposed to "reward men with sex". Here we have an answer that takes blame for all promiscuity off of women and places it all upon men. While there are certainly always scenarios that actually do exist in just about any category you can think of, including this one stated by the female author, the problem with making this a general statement in applying it to all men and all women, is imbalanced and lacking proper perspective.

The idea that men are "rewarded" with sex by women has not been an idea taught to all of us in our lives and one should not attempt to be speaking for everyone. My wife upon hearing the statement as she viewed the program with me also recognized the imbalance within it.

Her response to the author's statements was to say that if a woman believes sex is always a reward for the males only, she needs counseling to determine why she has no sex drive of her own or to find out why she has been misled about it.

A Biblical Admonition to Spouses

In Bible scripture, it is stated clearly that sexual relations between men and women who are spouses, is a co-equal reward and that it should never be denied to either the man or the woman.

I Cortinthians 7:3-5: *"The husband should fulfill his wife's sexual needs, and the wife should fulfill her husband's needs. The wife gives authority over her body to her husband, and the husband gives authority over his body to his wife. Do not deprive each other of sexual relations, unless you both agree to refrain from sexual intimacy for a limited time so you can give yourselves more completely to prayer. Afterward, you should come together again so that Satan won't be able to tempt you because of your lack of self-control."* (NLT)

Dangling Meat in front of Lions

The woman author also made the point during the interview that men are highly visually sexually-stimulated (a true statement that also applies to some women) and that women who wear provocative clothing, are in essence "dangling raw meat in front of lions". She also said that after a while those lions will "lash out to get that meat". Again, while there is an element of truth to this statement as well, it should be understood that only a certain percent of women dress provocatively and not just any woman will draw enticement from men by doing so. Women can be highly attractive, moderately attractive, mildly attractive or what we refer-to as being "homely".

This is not stated, to offend, it is simply a truth of life. I believe I speak for other men as well as myself, by pointing out that we grow tired of it being implied, that we are enticed by any and every woman, no matter who she is or the type of physical appearance she has because this is logically not true.

John Wayne made a statement to a woman in the movie "Hondo", saying to the effect, as the character of the same name, that some women think that every man who comes along wants them. I personally believe that most men have a bit more self control than that.

One of the men on the panel, being interviewed along with the woman-author, was a former porn addict and I believe such combinations on an interview panel, simply serves to enforce the idea that all men are the same and that all women are the same. According to statistics by some psychiatric sexual behavior studies and research reporting groups (i.e. The Pure Intimacy Organization and Dr. Patrick Carnes), 20% of sexual addicts are female this also means that 80% are not. You will not see such counter-balance statistics being stated when sexual addiction experienced by men is being discussed.

Are Sex and Intimacy Synonymous?

A final point the woman on the interview panel made, that I would also like to address briefly, is her statement that women who do seek sex, are actually seeking love, romance and intimacy.

I feel these type statements that are supposed to apply to all women, are also over-generalized because this obviously is not the case with every promiscuous woman or for women-in general for that matter. Again, I want to express that I do not add remarks like the ones that follow, to be offensive but I feel there should be more perspective added when these type blanket statements are made. My statements are these:

"Were the women in recent news coverage, who were convicted of being child molesters also seeking love and acceptance?"

"Were the women who molested the girls at the school founded by a famous media host, also simply seeking love and romance?"

I add these type statements in attempt to bring balance to what seems at times, to be a barrage of imbalanced views in regard to sexuality being applied to both men and women. The reason I direct my points more-so at the gender stereotypes, is because not many other people are doing so. This helps in turn, to bring better perspective in regard to the males or females these types of biased or prejudicial ideas and statements are directed at.

The Societal Evolution of Male Stereotypes

Raising a Husband Properly

Another Christian interview show I viewed recently, that featured another female author as a guest made similar statements. I suspected in the case of what was stated by her on this particular program, that she has been seriously hurt by men during her lifetime and as a result, she has possibly developed some resentment toward them in-general.

I base this on the fact that she made statements to the effect that women have to train men to act normally and that they must be taught by women to not be self-centered, self-seeking etc...

I questioned in my mind upon hearing these statements, as to whether she was implying that all women have pure motives at all times and that all men have impure ones at all times? This was not misunderstood on my part; the statements were expressed plainly and specifically.

My wife, who also watched this program with me, saw blatant imbalance in the statements this woman author was making.

Bombarded with Stereotypical Humor

I wish these were rare occurrences but they have actually been occurring, from my observation, for at least 30 years in mainstream media and for the most part, they go unchallenged by the males it is often directed at. Male stereotypes have also become a major mainstay of humor in movies and on television shows as well. Moronic males that are contrasted by sly seductive females, is replayed over and over again on shows, movies, commercials etc... and apparently is a point of humor that never grows old, otherwise it would not be presented for humorous effect as often as it is.

I'll end this chapter by saying that I absolutely adore women. I am the product of the union of a male and female (mom and dad) and so I'm a product of the womb and much of what I am comes from my mother as well as my father. How could I possibly resent or hate what is a part of me? I love women and they are my own flesh and blood, including my daughter, granddaughter, mother, grandmothers and my wife.

I respect and glorify women every chance I get but at some point, there simply has to be statements made to help offset the stereotypes that continue to be perpetrated toward the males of our society. It is simply a matter of trying to bring a bit of balance to these subjects.

Disappointment and resentment for continually being placed into general categories is a natural response if one really cares about societal perceptions and consequences. In-short, it gets really old over time and it's about time some of the over-generalizing is pointed out, with some balance and perspective added along the way.

CHAPTER FIVE

Biblical Commentary on Gender Bashing

Gender stereotyping remains prominent in our society to this day. Clearly, one effect this has is to degrade mankind in-general, so that they cannot as adequately operate in their God-given positions as leaders within their Churches and families. Following is a scripture, describing men who are to be Church and family leaders. These are the features of what the Bible calls "godly men", that much of the world seemingly no longer recognizes.

I Timothy 3:1-13:

1 This is a true saying, If a man desire the office of a bishop (church leader), he desireth a good work.

2 A bishop then must be blameless, the husband of one wife, vigilant, sober, of good behaviour, given to hospitality, apt to teach;

3 Not given to wine, no striker, not greedy of filthy lucre; but patient, not a brawler, not covetous;

The Societal Evolution of Male Stereotypes

4 One that ruleth well his own house, having his children in subjection with all gravity;

5 (For if a man know not how to rule his own house, how shall he take care of the church of God?)

6 Not a novice, lest being lifted up with pride he fall into the condemnation of the devil.

7 Moreover he must have a good report of them which are without; lest he fall into reproach and the snare of the devil.

8 Likewise must the deacons be grave, not doubletongued, not given to much wine, not greedy of filthy lucre;

9 Holding the mystery of the faith in a pure conscience.

10 And let these also first be proved; then let them use the office of a deacon, being found blameless.

11 Even so must their wives be grave, not slanderers, sober, faithful in all things.

12 Let the deacons be the husbands of one wife, ruling their children and their own houses well.

The Societal Evolution of Male Stereotypes

13 For they that have used the office of a deacon well purchase to themselves a good degree, and great boldness in the faith which is in Christ Jesus."

Obviously, if the world with the help of Satan (called "god of this world" in 2Corinthians 4:4) can constantly and consistently degrade the image of men and women, it begins to appear as if there are no godly men or women left to take these positions of authority and leadership in Church and family and therefore they also cannot be the protectors and leaders in our society.

Male Bashing Takes the Lead

There have also always been negative images and ideas wrongfully perpetrated about women as well as men, but never to the degree that the "male bashing" trend has been doing for many years. The "generalizing" of women into certain categories that are degrading to them in general, in my opinion, has never reached the same level of the ongoing male bashing trend.

Some might say that the view perpetrated by some, of women being "sex objects" would be an example from the other side of the coin.

Although this is also certainly a very wrong view to express, it is not quit the same thing. Women, who are interviewed, for being in the erotic related industry for example, have often commented that being desired sexually is "empowering". My point being, that although it is very wrong to view women as sex objects, you can't make that comparison, to the moronic type images men are placed into, when they are all stereotyped as "sex maniacs" (certainly some are in this category) and the many other negative views they are labeled with repeatedly.

MEN HAVE NOT BEEN DEFENDING AGAINST "MALE BASHING"

Although I cannot fully explain why, very few men have ever tried to defend against the male bashing phenomena over the years and mainly they have just sat back quietly and have "taken it". I believe this is partly due to the fact that men generally are not as open for discussion in these areas as women are and they don't desire to debate these issues because only "whiney wimps" complain, instead of taking it like a man. It is because of this in my opinion that "male bashing", especially in the area of sexuality has increased expediently for many years.

The Societal Evolution of Male Stereotypes

The fairly recently popularized remark stating that; "men just don't get it" (mentioned previously), which was in reference to men not realizing when they are being sexually harassing toward women, is an example of this generalizing and stereotyping of men. The fact is, there are still men in the world today, who "do get it" and are respectful to others and do not take part in sexually harassing women.

Some men also attest to being led by God in their lives, as he guides them through their conscience by His Spirit.

Romans 8:14: *"For as many as are led by the Spirit of God, they are the sons of God."*

MEN REPRESENTED AS SEXUAL MORONS

Even in movies and T.V. commercials, there has been, and is an image being perpetrated (although usually for comedic purposes), of men being completely moronic in the area of sexuality. Again, as I stated before, there is always truth to these things, for a percent of individuals however, these perpetrated images and ideas about men, are taken to extremes and touted continually.

The resulting effect is that the entire male side of the human race, is stereotyped and the trend has then gone too-far to be reversed. Women, who claim men deserve this type bashing, should consider the fact that any men they may truly love and respect may also be placed into these categories, such as their fathers, husbands, brothers etc... and even great men that have accomplished wonderful things for both men and women, including religious male figures, who represent their faith and worship.

To repeat, I realize that these types of overly-generalized views are also perpetrated against women. I am fully aware of that, so this part of the chapter is not meant to say that I believe it only happens to the male gender (more prominent but not exclusive). I simply wish to address these particular areas, because they are seldom addressed and also because I am male and wish to defend from the male viewpoint, as I should.

When men are continually told they are a certain way or fall within a certain negative category, without God's leading, they will begin to emulate those ungodly traits.

Proverbs 23:7: *"For as he thinketh in his heart, so is he..."*

The Societal Evolution of Male Stereotypes

TOO MANY MALE GENERALIZATIONS

The views I am describing about men are imbalanced by the fact that too many "generalizations" are used as previously mentioned. Men are sometimes placed into certain categories and are all stereotyped as being the same, in regard to wrongful acts or motives committed by some men, much of this being in the area of sexual offenses. When this same thing is done in regard to women, even in regard to less offensive issues, cries of outrage sometimes result because women feel degraded by comments that they feel includes all of them, rather than being directed toward the perpetrators of wrongful acts or motives that are being pointed out. Why would this not also be the case with men?

Listing examples is the best way to illustrate how the generalizing of men has been happening for many decades. As far as any motives for why this has been taking place, in addition to those I have already stated, I believe there are likely many motives. Another one that also comes to mind is the attempt by particular activist groups, to diminish the authority and leadership of men because it is seemingly perceived as unfair for men to be in this role.

In reality however, it is evident even in nature itself that the males of most species fulfill a role of leadership and authority, for the sake of family and also extending into other areas such as territory (country and freedom).

This does not in my opinion; diminish the extreme importance of the female role, for being in their positions of leadership and authority as well.

Ephesians 5:23- 28: *"For the husband is the head of the wife even as Christ is the head of the church, his body, and is himself its Savior. Now as the church submits to Christ, so also wives should submit in everything to their husbands.*

Husbands, love your wives, as Christ loved the church and gave himself up for her, that he might sanctify her, having cleansed her by the washing of water with the word, so that he might present the church to himself in splendor, without spot or wrinkle or any such thing, that she might be holy and without blemish. So ought men to love their wives as their own bodies. He that loves his wife loves himself."

The Societal Evolution of Male Stereotypes

MEN ONLY WANT "ONE THING"?

In giving this next example, I will point out a generalized view having to do with men seeking relationships with women, which naturally begins before he reaches adult age. The generalization in this area that has been applied to men in-general, for as long as I can recall during my lifetime is the view, that "men only want one thing". Notice that these remarks like the others I will address following, encompass the entire male side of the human race. I would not argue the fact that men were given a dominant sex drive and there are some who do seemingly want only one thing. I also will not argue the fact that during youth, human beings tend to only concentrate on the more basic needs and urges they have however this could be said of both sexes and not just males. Also, a dominant sex drive does not necessarily mean a stronger one but one that arises due to more triggers and one that occurs with more frequency. Obviously the reason for this, is the perpetuation of all species through pro-creation and if you feel it should not occur in this manner, take it up with The Creator, or mother nature, or whoever you feel is responsible for it (obviously this writer believes it was by God's design).

This aspect of male sexuality, is greatly expanded upon by those who wish to use it to degrade males generally and they will include into this view, the idea that all men are animalistic and only seeking self-gratification (certainly true of some). They also state that men are only interested in "the act" of intimacy and do not have desires for affection or romance. As I have echoed with each of these points, I'll again say this is true of some males but it is also true of some females, although a smaller percent of them. It is however; wrong to make this a general view of either gender. Most of mankind has temptations in these areas but there are lots of people in this world, who are not fornicators or adulterers.

There are men who also care very much about the affection aspect of their relationship and in having romantic experiences. Unfortunately, society says that it makes men "sissies" to admit this. Many men also care greatly about having deeper relationships with their wives, rather than just sexual ones. All men do not want "just one thing". There are some men with very strong sex drives, others with moderate sex drives and those with non-existent sex drives and everything in-between!

The Societal Evolution of Male Stereotypes

48

Recent statistics state that there are as many as thirty-million impotent men in the USA, which in-part accounts for the huge increase in prescriptions of erectile dysfunction drugs. Are these men also included among those who only want one thing?

Unfortunately, some who have always perpetrated the view that "all men" are a certain way regarding their sexual relationships, will also resort to degrading remarks, such as "men are dogs or pigs when it comes to sex" or "all men are perverts" etc..., I have heard these type statements directed at males in-general, all of my life.

Every adult person on earth, with very few exceptions, is guilty of what the Bible calls "adultery from their hearts" (Matthew 5:28) but not everyone is a "servant" to this physical lifestyle, as an actual life-practice.

There are also those who previously practiced fornication but have since become "new creatures in Christ" (II Corinthians 5:17) and after being "born again" (John 3:3) by God's Spirit and with his help, they no longer practice this type lifestyle.

The Societal Evolution of Male Stereotypes

ALL MEN ARE CAPABLE OF SEXUAL ABUSE?

Another area this generalizing has expanded into is the view, that all men are capable of committing rape or molestation. Some research groups have even conducted surveys of young men, asking them if they would commit rape, if they could get away with it and not be caught. I would propose that many surveys of these types are conducted, with a "predisposed outcome" desired. One can take just about any subject and skew the questions in such a way so-as to achieve the desired result. I'll also mention another factor not often considered. Did you know that males, many times will claim certain things or admit to certain things, out of concern that if they don't; it takes away from their masculinity (machismo)?

Rape is an act of violence and also an act of gaining submission from the victim, so that the perpetrator feels empowered. In saying all men are capable of raping women, one must understand that this requires a man to be violent to a woman and aroused at the same time. Did you know that there are men who are literally incapable of putting those two things together?

In other words, there are actually men who could not violently assault a woman and be sexually aroused at the same time. Rape is committed by men who are of a particular type and who are capable of this. The horrendous act of date rape by use of knock-out drugs is somewhat less of an act of violence but still requires that the perpetrator is capable of perverted tendencies.

The same is true of child molestation as well. I have seen television dialog shows in which Child Advocates will imply that all men are capable of this heinous crime. I completely agree that for the sake and safety of children, any stranger, male or female or anyone whosoever that acts inappropriately toward a child, should be considered by them as a potential danger because it is impossible for a child to know in advance, who might or might not be a danger to them. Children should be taught this precaution as soon as they are capable of understanding it.

Men, who are not capable of child molestation, cannot fathom being attracted sexually to a child. I have cited these examples to point out that men should not be generalized as having these tendencies in-general.

Males more often commit child molestation than do females and this is obviously a well-established fact statistically. The points I have attempted to express in these paragraphs, is to express the fact that regardless of how serious or significantly widespread a societal problem might be, it still does not include everyone and it is improper to generalize, by placing all males or all females into same categories regarding sexual offenses.

SEXUAL DEVIANCE IS NEVER PERPETRATED BY FEMALES?

Another area, in which I have had experience that goes against the "world's" generalized view of men, is that which stems from the idea that "it is always boys who pressure girls into sex". Experiences in my youth revealed to me, that girls are very much capable of pressuring boys into sex, although obviously less-often than the reverse scenario. My first steady girlfriend, whom I mentioned in a previous chapter became frustrated with me for not "getting serious" with her.

I was raised in a Christian home and was taught about the seriousness and possible consequences that pre-marital sex could cause me and this was the conviction I had for not giving in to it.

In Genesis Chapter thirty nine of the Bible, we see one of the earliest recorded incidents of a woman being a sexual predator toward a young man. The wife of a military leader in Egypt named Potiphar, persistently pursued Joseph, after the Bible says "she lusted after him with her eyes". She eventually, physically grabbed him at one point, by his cloths and he had to flee from her, by slipping out of his garment and running out of the room naked. She felt scorned by him because of this and told a false story to her husband, reversing the roles of what had actually occurred, stating that it was Joseph who had attacked her. He ended up in prison because of this, due to the false accusation.

Another Bible scripture states that "there is nothing new under the sun..." (Ecclesiastes 1:9). Some panelists on television dialog shows have stated that women are never predators and are never the ones who pursue the opposite sex.

53

In reality; men do not report being pursued or harassed, as often as women do, for fear of possible stigmas being attached. Despite this fact, males are far more often the perpetrators. This still does not mean that all men are sexual predators or harassers as some gender advocates have been implying for many years.

Genesis 39:7-20:

"And it came to pass after these things that his master's wife cast longing eyes on Joseph, and she said, 'Lie with me.' But he refused and said to his master's wife, 'Look, my master does not know what is with me in the house, and he has committed all that he has to my hand. There is no one greater in this house than I, nor has he kept back anything from me but you, because you are his wife. How then can I do this great wickedness, and sin against God?' So it was, as she spoke to Joseph day by day, that he did not heed her, to lie with her or to be with her. But it happened about this time, when Joseph went into the house to do his work, and none of the men of the house was inside, that she caught him by his garment, saying, 'Lie with me.'...

The Societal Evolution of Male Stereotypes

...

But he left his garment in her hand, and fled and ran outside. And so it was, when she saw that he had left his garment in her hand and fled outside, that she called to the men of her house and spoke to them, saying, 'See, he has brought in to us a Hebrew to mock us. He came in to me to lie with me, and I cried out with a loud voice. And it happened, when he heard that I lifted my voice and cried out, that he left his garment with me, and fled and went outside.' So she kept his garment with her until his master came home. Then she spoke to him with words like these, saying, 'The Hebrew servant whom you brought to us came in to me to mock me; so it happened, as I lifted my voice and cried out, that he left his garment with me and fled outside'. So it was, when his master heard the words which his wife spoke to him, saying, 'Your servant did to me after this manner,' that his anger was aroused. Then Joseph's master took him and put him into the prison, a place where the king's prisoners were confined. And he was there in the prison.''

(God blesses Joseph, in spite of the false accusation and he is freed and later becomes a ruler in Egypt.)

The Societal Evolution of Male Stereotypes

MEN CARE DEEPLY ABOUT PROTECTION AGAINST SEXUAL OFFENDERS

My intention in this final chapter was not to be offensive. The crimes of child molestation, sexual abuse of women and sexual harassment, are horrible crimes. Those of us men, who care very much about the victims of these crimes and in protecting our society against these type things, do not wish to be placed into the same categories, with those who commit them. We also do not wish to see these crimes perpetrated against the women we love or against anyone else for that matter.

It is obviously wrong to stereotype and generalize about men or women in regard to these types of societal issues. We must remember that there are many respectful men and women, who faithfully fulfill their roles of leadership, parenting and spousal duties in this world and they should be respectfully recognized and honored for doing so.

(END)